101
ESSENTIAL TIPS

Home Brewing

101

ESSENTIAL TIPS

Home Brewing

DK UK and US

Senior Editor	Chauney Dunford
Senior Art Editor	Clare Marshall
US Editor	Jill Hamilton
US Senior Editor	Shannon Beatty
Managing Editor	Penny Warren
Jacket Designer	Kathryn Wilding
Senior Pre-production Producer	Tony Phipps
Senior Producer	Ché Creasey
Art Director	Jane Bull
Publisher	Mary Ling

DK INDIA

Project Editor	Nidhilekha Mathur
Senior Art Editor	Balwant Singh
Art Editor	Aparajita Barai
DTP Designers	Manish Chandra Upreti, Rajdeep Singh
Senior Picture Researcher	Sumedha Chopra
Managing Editor	Alicia Ingty
Managing Art Editor	Navidita Thapa
Pre-production Manager	Sunil Sharma

US Consultant	Michael Foran

First American edition 2015
Published in the United States by
DK Publishing
345 Hudson Street, New York, New York 10014

A Penguin Random House Company

15 16 17 18 19 10 9 8 7 6 5 4 3 2 1
001-274504-May/2015

A catalog record for this book is available from the Library of Congress.

ISBN 978-1-4654-3004-5

DK books are available at special discounts when purchased in bulk for sales
promotions, premiums, fund-raising, or educational use. For details, contact:
DK Publishing Special Markets, 345 Hudson Street, New York, New York 10014
or SpecialSales@dk.com.

Printed and bound in China at South China Printing Co Ltd

A WORLD OF IDEAS
SEE ALL THERE IS TO KNOW

www.dk.com

101 ESSENTIAL TIPS

INGREDIENTS

GETTING STARTED

Pages 50 to 55
RECIPES

Pages 56 to 69
THE NEXT LEVEL

WHAT IS BEER?

1

HISTORY OF BEER

Beer has been around for almost as long as mankind has grown grain. It is impossible to establish who invented beer or when that happened, but evidence shows that the first beer was brewed around 5000 BCE.

Sumerian women of ancient Mesopotamia (present-day Iraq) brew the first beer. This was most likely produced from a mash made of soaked bread, left to ferment in open containers.

Traces of beer found in the offerings made to the Pharaohs in the tombs of Egypt indicate that beer was a sacred drink. It is also believed that common people, including children, drank beer during this period as a source of nutrition.

During the Viking age (800–1000 CE), beer was considered an important beverage in the Nordic countries to accompany the salty food (salt was used as a food preservative then), as well as a healthier alternative to water, which was unfit for consumption. Beer, ale in particular, with its lower alcohol content, was drunk on a regular basis, while mead, fermented honey with water, with its higher alcohol content, was enjoyed at festive events.

| 5000 BCE | 1800 BCE | 1550 BCE | 800 BCE | 800–1000 | 1040 |

The oldest beer recipe in the world evolves. Called the "Hymn to Ninkasi," goddess of beer for the Sumerians, the hymn was both a prayer and a clever way to remember a beer recipe.

Women emerge as the first brewers in Germany.

In ancient Greece and Italy, beer was considered a drink for barbarians—this attitude influenced the rest of Europe as well.

Christian monks develop modern brewing technology and beer is sold from monasteries. The well-educated monks also improved the brewing technology, particularly with regard to sanitation facilities, and meticulously recorded and refined their recipes.

Monks also add hops to beer, making it possible to preserve it during long excursions.

Fresh hop cones

DEFINING BEER

2

Beer is a fermented, alcoholic beverage made from water, malt, hops, and yeast. However, it can also be nonalcoholic or contain additional ingredients, such as fruit and spices. It is the third most popular beverage in the world, after water and tea. There are two main categories of beer: ale and lager. The two differ in color, taste, and smell due to the difference in the type of yeast used for making them (see Tip 6). The process of making beer is called brewing, which involves five main steps: malting, mashing, boiling, fermenting, and conditioning.

Traditional German beer stein

Brewer's yeast

Engish bitter

The lager originates in Bavaria (now a state in Germany) when brewers experiment by storing beer at a lower temperature, often in caves, for a longer period, allowing the yeast to settle. This technique gave the beer an additional freshness and a higher level of carbon dioxide. It also extended its shelf life.

The marriage of Crown Prince Ludwig held in Munich, Germany is commemorated by a festival that goes on to become the famous Oktoberfest beer festival.

Louis Pasteur discovers yeast and its role in fermentation, allowing brewers to control how they ferment their beers.

The beer world continues to grow as more and more home brewers experiment with different yeast strains and techniques to create their own unique styles of beer.

| 1200 | 1516 | 1810 | 1842 | 1857 | 1971 | 1990– PRESENT |

The "Reinheitsgebot," also known as the "German Beer Purity Law," is established in Bavaria to guarantee the quality of beer and also to avoid competition from bakers using wheat and rye. The law states that brewers are only allowed to use water, barley, and hops when producing beer. Yeast was not known at that time and was added to the list at a later stage.

The first golden lager is produced in Pilsen, Bohemia.

Barley grains

English journalists Michael Hardman, Graham Lees, Bill Mellor, and Jim Maken discuss setting up a consumer organization for beer drinkers. This later becomes Campaign for Real Ale (CAMRA).

Real ale

HARD AND SOFT WATER
The mineral content differentiates hard water from soft water—hard water has a higher concentration of calcium and magnesium.

3 WATER

Water, referred to as "liquor" in brewing, is the main ingredient in beer. Since the water profile varies according to the water source, breweries traditionally adapted their beers to the local water supply. That is why some beer styles are more common in certain areas, such as stout, which is best made using the hard water available in Dublin, Ireland. In general, soft water is better suited for lighter beer styles, such as Pilsner, while hard water is better suited for darker beer styles, such as ale and stout.

4 GRAIN

The grain generally used in brewing is barley, although other grains, such as wheat or rye, can also be used. For use in brewing, grain is converted into "malt" through a process called "malting." Malting involves extracting starch from the grain, which is then converted into sugar during the process of mashing (see Tip 42). The malting process is divided into four steps; steeping, germination, drying, and roasting. In steeping, raw barley is soaked in water for a couple of days. Then it is gradually dried at an even temperature while being aerated to allow the barley to germinate. Once the husks open and germination is complete, the sprouting process is halted by drying the barley. The dried malt can then be roasted in a number of ways to bring out certain characteristics (see Tip 32).

GROWING BARLEY
The "two-row" barley is the most common barley variety used in brewing due to its high starch content.

OTHER BREWING GRAINS
Apart from barley, other cereal grains, such as wheat and rye, can also be used to brew beer. Typically, a percentage of these grains is mixed with barley to brew the beer.

Wheat grains   Rye grains

GROWING HOP BINES
Hop bines can grow over 20 ft (6 m) tall, and are grown over stringed supports. The strings can be lowered during harvesting, allowing the cones from the tallest plants to be collected easily.

5 BITTERING

The primary bittering agent used in beer is hops. The hop plant is a vine grown up stringed supports that are some 10 feet high. The hops used in brewing are the flowers of the female hop plant. Hop flowers were also used medically to induce sleep due to their calming effect. However, they are probably more renowned for their antibacterial and preserving capabilities, which led to the development of IPA (India Pale Ale), because the hops kept the beer fresh during the long voyage from Great Britain to India. Hops contain oils with alpha acids, which exude when boiling and give the beer its bitterness. The longer the hops are boiled, the more bitter the beer. Hops also add aroma and flavor depending on when they are added in the brewing process (see Tip 51).

6 YEAST

Saccharomyces cerevisiae is the species of yeast used in baking and brewing. In brewing, yeast is generally divided into two categories: ale yeast and lager yeast. Ale yeast ferments at a higher temperature than lager yeast. Although yeast is primarily added to the brew to transform sugar into alcohol, it also controls the flavor profile of the beer. So, choose a yeast strain according to the style of beer you are aiming for (see Tip 82).

YEAST IN BREWING
Prior to Louis Pasteur's discovery of yeast in 1857, brewers simply left their wort (the mixture of water and grain) uncovered, letting wild yeast spores in the air ferment their brew.

11

VIENNA LAGER
The fermentation time and temperature distinguishes this Vienna lager from the top-fermented beers.

7 BOTTOM-FERMENTED BEER

This is beer brewed with lager yeast (see Tip 6), which means that it is fermented at a lower temperature, generally around 45–57°F (7–14°C), and takes longer to ferment. Just as the name indicates, the yeast falls to the bottom of the vessel during the fermentation process. Some of the beer types that fall under this category are lager, bock, and pilsner.

Lager   Bock   Pilsner

8 TOP-FERMENTED BEER

This is beer brewed with ale yeast and fermented at a higher temperature than a lager, normally around 63–75°F (17–23°C). Contrary to lager yeast, the ale yeast rises to the surface during fermentation and develops a thick foam head on top of the beer. Bitter, stout, and India Pale Ale (IPA) are examples of top-fermented beers in the ale category.

BELGIAN GOLDEN STRONG ALE
This Belgian golden strong ale is fermented using the ale yeast, Wyeast Belgian ale with yeast number 1214.

Bitter   Stout   India Pale Ale (IPA)

SPONTANEOUSLY FERMENTED BEER

9

A spontaneously fermented beer is one where no yeast has been added. The beer ferments using yeast that naturally occurs in the air, often giving a sour-tasting beer. However, this fermentation process is not for the impatient, because the process can take up to a year.

LAMBIC BEER
Brewed in Belgium, the wort for lambic beers is exposed to the wild yeasts and bacteria native to the Zenne valley, in which Brussels lies. This is what gives these beers their distinctive dry and vinous flavor, usually with a sour aftertaste.

Lambic ale

OPEN FERMENTATION
An open fermenter is used to expose the wort to airborne yeast spores. No additional yeast is added.

10 THREE DIFFERENT BREWING METHODS

Home brewers have a choice of three different brewing methods:
brewing kit, malt extract, and all-grain brewing, also known as
full-mash brewing. All three methods are described below.

BREWING KIT

This is the simplest method of brewing beer at home. The kit already contains the finished
wort—the mix of grains and hops—so only water and yeast is to be added. Once the beer
has fermented, it is poured into bottles. Before you begin, read the instructions and
recommendations from the manufacturer carefully. This method is perfect for beginners who
want to brew their own beer but with minimum effort and mess. However, the beer made
from a brewing kit is not comparable to beer that has been brewed at home using the
all-grain brewing method because no alterations are possible in an already-prepared recipe.

1 Place the malt cans from the kit in a pan
of warm water to soften the malt. Then
empty the contents into your fermenter and
add a kettleful of boiling water.

2 Add cold water to make up the required
volume, then stir vigorously to oxygenate
the wort and encourage fermentation. Take
a gravity reading of the wort (see Tip 47).

3 Now dip a thermometer into the wort
and take a temperature reading. If the
temperature is more than 75°F (24°C),
close the lid and wait for it to cool because
otherwise you will kill the yeast cells. The
ideal temperature required varies according
to the type of yeast you are using and the
style of beer you are brewing.

4 Open the yeast packet and sprinkle
the yeast over the surface of the wort.
Check the manufacturer's instructions
for any other ingredient to be added at
this stage. Put the lid on the fermenter,
fit an airlock (see Tip 61), and leave to
ferment. Then follow Tips 62–72.

MALT EXTRACT

This is a slightly advanced method where you have a prepared malt extract, but can add hops to the beer. The malt extract comes either as liquid malt or spray malt. Using this method means skipping the mashing process (see Tip 42), which saves around 2 hours. This method is good if you want to create your own beer, but still want to keep it simple and easy. However, this method does not allow as many malt variations as the all-grain brewing method.

1 Measure out all ingredients, including hops, and sterilize all your equipment. Measure the required volume of water into a boiler and heat it. If the recipe calls for steeped grains (see Step 2), then heat the water to 158°F (70°C), otherwise bring it to a boil and jump to step 3.

2 Add the grains to the boiler using a grain bag, if you have one, and leave to infuse for 30 minutes. Maintain the temperature at 149–158°F (65–70°C). Strain the grains, or remove the bag, and bring the water to a boil.

3 Remove the pan from the heat and add the malt extract. Stir well. Place the pan back on the heat and bring to a vigorous boil.

4 Add the hops for bittering and keep adding subsequent batches as per the recipe. Remember to add any flavor hops at the end of the boil. Cool the wort (see Tip 54), then transfer it to a fermenter. Then follow Tips 58–72.

ALL-GRAIN BREWING

This method requires more knowledge and equipment and takes a longer time, of approximately 4–6 hours. It involves a number of processes (see Tips 37–72), which give you the opportunity to affect the finished result. The kind of grain and hops, and the yeast strain you choose, all affect the beer you create. It is also very satisfying to learn the craft of brewing from the beginning.

EQUIPMENT

11 HAND SPRAYER

It is useful to have a household hand sprayer for sterilizing the equipment during the brewing process. An inexpensive model found in any supermarket will work just fine.

ACID-BASED STERILIZERS
Such sterilizers are easy to use, work quickly, and can be used on most materials, including stainless steel.

12 CLEANER AND STERILIZER

A cleaner is used to clean the equipment, while a sterilizer is used to kill bacteria. All brewing equipment needs to be both cleaned and sanitized before use, so invest in a good cleaner and sterilizer before you start brewing.

13 MEASURING CUP

The measuring cup should preferably be made out of steel or heatproof glass because it is easier to sterilize a steel or glass cup by boiling. If using a plastic one, sterilize it with a sterilizer. To save time and minimize errors when measuring, choose a measuring cup that can measure up to at least 1¾ pints (one liter).

Glass measuring cup

Digital timer

14 COOKING TIMER

The cooking timer can be analog or digital, although a digital one is better as it tends to be more exact. The timer is used during the mashing process (see Tip 42) and while adding the hops to the mash (see Tip 51).

15 LARGE SPOON

A large spoon made of stainless steel or heat-resistant plastic is useful for stirring the wort. It is also possible to use a brewing paddle, although not essential.

PLASTIC SPOON
Use a plastic spoon if you have a plastic fermenter or container for brewing because it will be less likely to scratch the container.

Stainless steel spoon

16 THERMOMETER

Several types of thermometers are available, but the main ones are analog thermometers, that is, glass spirit thermometers, and digital thermometers. It is safer to use a digital thermometer because the glass of an analog thermometer can break. The thermometer is used during several steps in the brewing process to monitor the temperature of the mash, the wort, as well as during fermentation. It's important that the thermometer can handle a temperature range of 32–230°F (0–110°C).

EASE OF USE
A digital thermometer is not only sturdy and exact, but it is also easier to see the temperature reading on it.

Digital thermometer

LARGE FINE-MESH SIEVE

A stainless steel sieve with a fine mesh is required to remove particles after the boil (see Tip 57). Preferably, buy one with a steel handle rather than a wooden one— wooden handles can get scratched or stained and may even bleed over a period of time. If you are using a fermenter with a small opening, such as a carboy, place a large funnel below the sieve while filtering to reduce splash.

Steel handle provides stability and is long-lasting

Fine mesh catches even tiny particles while filtering

CHOOSE WITH CARE

Choose a sieve with a long handle and a grip at the other end so you can easily position it on your fermenter. A regular kitchen sieve will also work, but be careful of hygiene.

A large bowl helps to measure light, but large-sized ingredients, such as hops

FOOD SCALES

Food scales are required for weighing most of the ingredients used in brewing, such as hops, yeast, grain, and sugar. You can use either an analog or a digital scale, but a digital one is preferred because it is easy to read. The individual hop batches may be very small or very large in size so get a scale that can measure in 15½ grain (1g) increments up to 10 lb (4.5kg).

KETTLE

You will need to heat water several times during the brewing process. A kettle can come in handy to quickly boil water; a simple stovetop kettle will work fine, but if you can find one, an electric kettle will be faster. The kettle can also be used to heat up water when sterilizing equipment (see Tip 38).

MARKS THE END OF FERMENTATION

The hydrometer and trial jar also help determine when fermentation is complete. If the readings remain the same over a period of 3–4 days, that means that your beer is fermented and you can move on to the next step in the process.

Trial jar

Hydrometer

20 HYDROMETER AND TRIAL JAR

A hydrometer is an instrument used to measure the gravity of a liquid. In other words, it measures the amount of sugar that is contained in the liquid. A high reading means the liquid has a high sugar content; a low reading means the sugar has turned to alcohol. A trial jar is a long, beakerlike jar that is used to collect a sample of the liquid to be measured. It can be made of either plastic or glass and is filled with a sample of the wort. The hydrometer is floated in the trial jar, which is calibrated to be used with liquids at room temperature, normally around 68°F (20°C), so make sure that your sample is at this temperature for an accurate reading.

TAKING THE READING

A hydrometer and trial jar is used several times during the brewing process to calculate the amount of alcohol in the finished beer.

When taking a reading, make sure that you read at eye level, at the same plane as the horizontal surface of the liquid, rather than at the point where the liquid rises as it touches the stem of the hydrometer. Also, make sure that the hydrometer does not touch the side of the trial jar.

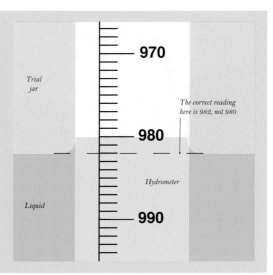

Trial jar

Liquid

970

980

The correct reading here is 982, not 980

Hydrometer

990

21 BOILING BAGS

You can use a boiling bag for putting your hops in when boiling to prevent unwanted particles from entering the wort. Both nylon and muslin bags work equally well, although if you are using hop pellets, use the finer-meshed nylon bags. Make sure that you leave some room in the bag to allow the hops or hop pellets, if using, to expand. Boiling bags can also be used when dry hopping (see Tip 89).

EASE OF USE
Boiling bags are easy to lower into the vessel and to lift out after use.

22 BOILING POT

You will need a boiling pot in which to boil a large volume of liquid. A number of boiling pots are available in the market; you can choose from stainless steel or ceramic boiling pots. Both of these are hard wearing and easy to clean. Whichever pot you buy, make sure that it is the right size for your recipe, typically 2¾–5¼ gallons (10–20 liters). Moreover, you also need to take into consideration that boiling liquid requires more space than cold, so always buy a pot that can hold more volume than the total quantity of your brew. Additionally, be careful not to use a size that exceeds the power output of your stovetop.

GO ELECTRIC
Some boilers come with a built-in heating element and need not be heated up on a stove.

Temperature settings

Stainless steel boiling pot

Plastic boiling pot

Airlock

Tap

Plastic fermenter

23 FERMENTATION VESSEL WITH AIRLOCK

A fermentation vessel is the container in which the wort ferments once yeast is added to it. There are many different types available, but the most common and inexpensive ones are plastic buckets or carboys. The fermenter needs to be an airtight vessel with an airlock, and it should be large enough to leave room for the fermentation process. For example, if you plan to ferment 5¼ gallons (20 liters), then you will require a vessel that can hold 8 gallons (30 liters). There are different fermentation methods, primary and secondary fermentation, and depending on which method you choose, you might need two vessels when fermenting (see Tip 62).

THE GLASS OPTION
Also known as a carboy, a glass fermenter is easy to clean, doesn't stain, and even allows you to see the beer as it ferments.

24 MASH TUN

A mash tun is a vessel where you combine crushed malt with hot water during the mash (see Tip 42). It should be insulated and fitted with a false bottom or bazooka screen, and a tap. The false bottom or bazooka screen functions as a sieve to filter out the wort and remove the peels and particles. Depending on which mashing method you use (see Tip 81), one or the other piece of equipment is preferred.

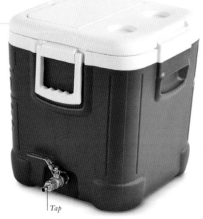

Tap

25 SIPHON

A siphon is used to transfer liquid from one vessel to another. A siphon can even be as simple as a length of plastic tubing. Some siphons also have a sediment trap at one end, which prevents residue from being sucked up, and a tap at the other end to control the flow. An auto siphon, which starts the siphon pump function without having to provide suction, may be more hygienic and easier to use.

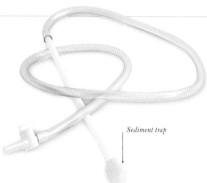

Sediment trap

26 MALT MILL

A malt mill is used for crushing the grain before it is added to the mash, although grains can also be bought precrushed. There is a wide price range of malt mills available on the market, from simple, cheap ones to expensive, professional ones (see Tip 94). The most important thing to keep in mind is that the malt should be crushed, not ground. If the malt has been ground to flour, the mashing process won't work.

Copper piping helps cool the wort at a fast rate

Plastic tubes connect the chiller to the cold water faucet

Immersion chiller

27 WORT CHILLER

A wort chiller is used to cool large volumes of hot wort quickly. It can be made of either coiled copper or stainless steel tubing, which is connected to the cold water faucet. When placed in the boiling pot, the cold water running through the coils helps cool the wort at a fast rate (see Tip 54). For a simpler and cost-effective solution, you can also fill a bucket or tub with ice to create an ice bath and immerse the pot in it (see Tip 55).

28 CROWN CAPPER

A crown capper is used to seal the bottles with a cap. There are two main variants of crown cappers: the manual bench crown capper, which is fixed on a bench and the bottle placed on it to fix the crown, and the twin lever capper, which is placed directly on the bottle to attach the crown. Both are good for home use to put crowns on glass bottles.

Twin lever capper

29 CAPS

Bottle caps come in different sizes and types. The most commonly used are the smaller size (1 in/26 mm) crown caps made of tin-plated steel. Make sure you sterilize the caps before use.

30 BOTTLES

When choosing beer bottles, pay attention to the color of the bottle because beer reacts to sunlight. Brown bottles are better than green or colorless ones because brown bottles filter out harmful light, which prevents the beer from going bad. Always sterilize the bottles before use. The beer can also be stored in plastic bottles, which are easy to handle and eliminate the need for a crown capper.

The dark color helps filter out sunlight and prevents the beer from developing off-flavors

BOTTLES WITH ATTACHED CAPS
Swing-top bottles are a great alternative if you want to save the hassle of using separate caps. They can also be easily resealed and look attractive.

INGREDIENTS

31 HOT LIQUOR

Water makes up 90–97% of the content in beer and is also known by brewers as the "liquor." Depending on where you live, water will have a certain characteristic, which may affect the quality and taste of your final product. If you want to brew a particular type of beer, you can treat the water to fit your requirement (see Tip 80).

USE HOT WATER
Heat the water to around 167–172°F (75–78°C). Make sure it is hot, not boiling, when you use it.

Whole malt grains

32 MALT

Malt is grain that has been treated in a process called "malting" (see Tip 4) for use in brewing. It provides fermentable sugars and adds flavor, color, and aroma to the beer. Several different types of malt are available, with pale ale malt, called base malt, and lightly roasted pilsner malt, being the most common. Unmalted malt, which is malt without any starch, is also used to add flavor and aroma to the beer.

BASE MALTS
Base malts make up the major portion of the "grain bill" – the sum of different grains that go into a recipe – and are mashed while brewing to provide the yeast with sugar.

Pale pilsner malt

Wheat malt

SPECIALTY MALTS
The main purpose of specialty malts, such as chocolate malt, is to add aroma and color to the beer. Caramel malt, amber malt, and roasted malt are all different kinds of specialty malt.

Caramel malt

Amber malt

Roasted malt

33 HOPS

Hops are the cone-shaped flowers of the female hop plant (see Tip 5), which are added to beer for bitterness, aroma, or flavor. A huge variety of hops is available, and most brewers mix different types of hops in the same batch to create a certain style of beer. Hops can be purchased fresh or dried. It is easy to distinguish fresh hops from dried hops by looking at the color, green is fresh and brown dried, but also judging by the aroma. Fresh hops have a spicy and fresh aroma while dried hops have a pungent, cheesy smell. Dried hops can last for years, if stored properly in an airtight container, without the aroma changing significantly.

HOP PELLETS
Hop pellets are pulverized and pressed hop cones. They are now often favored due to the consistency they bring when brewing, as well as their storage qualities.

Fresh hops

Dried hops

25

YEAST TYPES

34 Yeast is the ingredient that turns the sweet wort, produced from malt, hops, and water, into beer. It is available live (in liquid form) and dried. These forms are used in different ways to ferment the beer. It is important to read the instructions carefully on how the yeast should be used because it can vary between manufacturers.

LIQUID YEAST
This is cultured yeast and is generally of a higher quality than dried yeast. There is a wide range of liquid yeasts available to choose from.

DRIED YEAST
Dried yeast has a long shelf life and is easy to use. However, the range of dried yeast available can be quite limited.

CLEARING AGENT

35 Clearing agent, also known as fining agent, is used to reduce the cloudiness generally caused by proteins, tannins, and yeast in the beer. It works by preventing the proteins in the malt from being transferred to the fermenter. There are several brands available on the market, but most clearing agents contain the active component, carrageen. Some popular clearing agents include protafloc and Irish moss.

Protafloc   Irish moss

36

SUGAR

Sugar is used at two different stages in brewing; first to increase gravity when boiling (see Tip 48), and second to create carbon dioxide before bottling, called "priming" in brewing terminology (see Tip 67). Plain white table sugar is adequate. As a general rule, the more sugar you add, the higher the alcohol content of the beer will be, if matched with yeast that can consume that amount of sugar. Sugar can also be used to add flavor to the beer. A huge variety of sugar types is available, and all add their particular taste to the beer. Other sources of fermentable sugars include dried malt extract (DME) and liquid malt extract (LME).

Table sugar

CANDI SUGAR
Candi sugar is the cane sugar often used in Belgian beers. You can use the dark or the light type of candi sugar, both give different characteristics to the beer.

HONEY
Honey is a popular addition in home-brewed beers. The flavor and aroma varies depending on the region or the flower the nectar has been gathered from.

MOLASSES
Molasses, used by some home brewers, has a potent and aromatic flavor.

GETTING STARTED

37 CHOOSE A RECIPE

It is more complicated to succeed with lager than ale; therefore, it is advisable for beginners in general to start with brewing ale. Ale ferments at room temperature and no cooling of the wort (see Tip 54) is required. Lager, on the other hand, requires the wort to be cooled during fermentation, for which additional equipment is required (see Tip 55).

BREWING LAGERS
To brew a lager successfully, you not only require extra equipment, but must also be very careful about the fermentation conditions.

38 HYGIENE

In brewing, hygiene is of the utmost importance and should not be compromised under any circumstances. The beer can easily get contaminated through poor hygiene, particularly after the wort has been cooled down (see Tip 54), during fermentation (see Tip 62), and while bottling (see Tip 68). Before the boil (see Tip 49) hygiene is not as important since the boil will kill all bacteria. Always wash your hands thoroughly with soap before you start brewing. Clean all the work surfaces carefully. Set up a clean zone, such as a tray, to keep all the cleaned and sterilized equipment in so you don't mix them with the rest. The best and most environmentally friendly way to sterilize your equipment is by boiling it. However, this only works for smaller equipment that can withstand high temperatures and handling boiling water is both time-consuming and dangerous. You could also invest in a sterilizing liquid that works quickly and can be easily sprayed onto the equipment.

STERILIZING SMALL PIECES
For ease, sterilize small pieces of equipment by placing them inside the fermenter.

CLEANING BOTTLES
Wash out bottles as soon as the contents are finished to prevent the yeast sediment at the bottom of the bottles from drying up. If the bottles are very soiled, soak them in a light bleach solution for an hour. Then clean each bottle with a bottle brush to remove any debris. Sterilize and rinse the bottles for use.

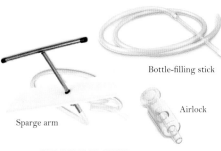

Bottle-filling stick

Airlock

Sparge arm

CLEANING PLASTIC
Don't clean plastic equipment too vigorously or scratch it while cleaning. It is best to replace plastic parts after heavy usage.

39 MEASURE MALT AND HOPS

Prepare for every step of the process in advance to avoid unnecessary errors when working under pressure and to help the brewing process go smoothly. Weigh every ingredient that you are using in advance. If you are using pre-milled malt, then the packet will tell you how much it weighs. Otherwise, take care to weigh the malt before milling it, using an accurate scale. You need to be fairly precise when weighing malt and even more so when weighing hops. The smaller the batch, the more exact you need to be. It is common to have several different types of hops in one batch or to have the same type of hop but added at different intervals. To avoid mixing them, place the different hops or different batches of the same hop in separate bowls or bags and tag them with the name of the hop and the time at which they should be added.

Amber malt

Pale malt

Flaked maize

Hops

Protafloc

MEASURING RIGHT
To get the right results, use a scale that measures in minute units (see Tip 18).

WEIGHING HOP PELLETS
Hop pellets are more concentrated than whole hops, so less is required. Keep this in mind when weighing the hop quantity.

40 MILL THE GRAIN

If you are not using pre-milled malt, then the malt grains will need to be milled using a malt mill. Take the measured malt and pour it into the malt mill to break open the corn. Be careful that the malt is milled rather than ground; otherwise, it will become flour and impossible to mash. The largely intact husk will be useful later on in wort filtration.

FINAL GRAIN TEXTURE
For the grain to be effective for brewing, the milled grain should resemble crushed, rather than ground grain.

CHECK THE WATER TEMPERATURE
Use a thermometer—a digital one works best—to check the temperature of the water before pouring it into the mash tun.

41 MEASURE AND HEAT WATER

Most recipes specify the amount of water, which brewers call "liquor," required for mashing. Carefully measure the required volume and heat it. The water should not be boiling when you pour it into the mash tun, but it should be at a temperature of around 167–172°F (75–78°C). The recipe will tell you the exact temperature. Pour the hot water into the mash tun, reserving some for later use.

42 MASHING

Add the crushed malt to the hot water in the mash tun. The temperature of the liquid, called the "mash," will drop to the "mash-in step temperature" as specified in the recipe. If the temperature goes lower than what has been specified, add some of the reserved hot water (see Tip 41), stirring as you pour. When the mash reaches the defined temperature, put the lid on and let it stand for about an hour, or as specified in the recipe. This step is called "mashing." Mashing releases the sugar and flavors from the malted barley to produce what is called the "wort." Check the mash from time to time to ensure that the correct temperature is maintained. If the temperature drops again, add some more of the reserved hot liquor.

POURING THE MALT
Pour the malt into the mash tun very slowly to avoid creating any lumps or dry areas.

WHAT IS MASHING?

Mashing is the process by which the starches in the malted grain are converted into fermentable sugars. The grains are steeped in hot water for about an hour to produce a sweet liquid called "wort."

31

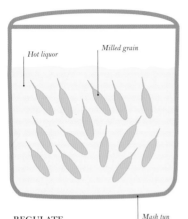

43 MASH TEMPERATURE

Keep the temperature of the mash as close to that specified in the recipe as possible, although a difference of up to one degree is acceptable. A lower temperature will result in a drier beer while a higher temperature will make the beer sweeter due to less fermentable sugar.

REGULATE TEMPERATURE
Keep measuring the temperature of the mash from time to time to ensure that it does not go above or below the target temperature.

Mash tun

TEMPERATURE FACTS

For the starch to convert to sugar the temperature needs to fall in the range of 144–160°F (62–71°C). To get a medium body, the temperature should be around 151°F (66°C), while a temperature over 162°F (72°C) will give a stringent taste to the malt.

44 RECIRCULATE THE WORT

Gently open the tap on the mash tun a little so that the "wort" starts to run out. Allow the wort to seep into a small container, such as a measuring cup. In the beginning, the wort that comes out will be cloudy and full of husk debris. Let the tap remain open during the entire process, but only a little bit. Carefully pour the cloudy wort back into the mash tun so that the wort is purified through the malt bed and repeat the process until the wort is completely clear. Be careful not to stir the wort during this process.

POUR GENTLY
Pour the recirculated wort very slowly back into the mash tun to avoid disturbing the malt bed. You can use a measuring cup, or even pour the wort onto a brewing spoon that is dipped into the wort to make the process smoother.

45 SPARGING

Sparging, or lautering, is a process that rinses out the sugar-rich wort from the malt by slowly running warm water through the malt bed. This process will take 20–30 minutes, so be patient. Start when the recirculated wort runs clear; set up a sparge arm, if using (see Tip 46), on top of the mash tun and allow warm water that is around 169–171°F (76–77°C) to spray over the wort. Then allow the wort to slowly drain into the boiling pot or use a measuring cup to pour the wort from the mash tun to the boiling pot. The easiest way, however, is to place the boiling pot beneath the mash tun and open the tap so that the wort can flow straight down into the boiling pot.

WORT STRENGTH
Add only as much water during sparging as is required to obtain the amount of wort specified in the recipe. Otherwise, you will not achieve the desired wort strength.

HOME BREWING SETUP
An easy way of facilitating the brewing process is to use three separate vessels—a hot liquor tank or HLT for heating and storing water, a mash tun for mixing the malt and hot water, and a boiling pot for boiling the wort with hops. Place the vessels one below the other to allow gravity to do the work for you without having to set up expensive equipment.

Hot liquor tank (HLT)

Mash tun

Boiling pot

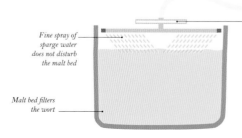

Fine spray of sparge water does not disturb the malt bed

Sparge arm rotates over the surface of the wort so that the spray of water is even

Malt bed filters the wort

CHECK THE MALT BED
The malt bed helps filter the wort, so do not turn it over or let it become dry during the lautering process.

46

SPARGING FACTS

Be very careful while sparging. If you sparge too much or if the temperature is too high, tannins will precipitate, resulting in tannic acid. This will give the finished beer a stringent flavor as well as affect its quality. On the contrary, if you sparge too little, the dilution of sugar in the wort will become stronger, but the amount of beer will be less. You can take a gravity reading of the hot wort to check the sugar content (see Tip 47).

VOLUME OF SPARGE WATER

The volume of sparge water to be added is usually mentioned in the recipe. This quantity is different from the volume of water used in mashing (see Tip 41).

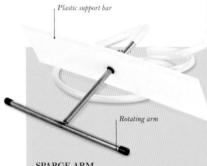

Plastic support bar

Rotating arm

SPARGE ARM

A sparge arm may be used for rinsing the grains during continuous sparging (see Tip 45), although a lot of home brewers also sparge without it as well. A sparge arm works like a sprinkler, using a hollow, perforated stainless steel tube that rotates freely when water flows through it. A support bar on top helps position the sparge arm across the top of the mash tun.

SPARGING METHODS

There are three main methods of sparging that home brewers can use.

Continuous sparging is where a fine spray of water is added continuously to the surface of the wort, while an equal amount of wort is drained from the bottom of the mash tun. This method extracts the most amount of sugar from the grains.

In batch sparging, the entire amount of sparge water is added to the mash. The mash is stirred, then left to infuse for 20 minutes. A small amount of wort is run off and then returned to the mash to filter any grain debris, until the runoff is clear. Then the wort is drained into the boiler and the process repeated.

The no-sparge method, as its name indicates, is where no sparge water is added and the wort is run directly into the boiling pot. Although this is the easiest method, a lot of sugar is left behind.

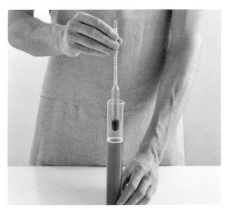

USING THE HYDROMETER
Hold the hydrometer above the trial jar, then lower it into the wort sample. When the hydrometer reaches its point of equilibrium, let it go, then wait for it to settle. If bubbles obscure the scale, gently turn the stem to release them.

47 CONTROL WORT DENSITY

Once the sparging water is running low or just a little water is left in the sparging tank, it is time to check how much sugar the wort contains. Take a clean trial jar and fill it up directly from the tap on the mash tun. Check the reading using a hydrometer (see Tip 20). The level must not fall below 1010 on the scale of the hydrometer to avoid the development of tannins. You can also check the gravity reading of the hot wort using a refractometer (see Tip 99).

48 ADJUST THE TARGETED ALCOHOL LEVEL

There is no alcohol in the wort at this stage, so, depending on the alcohol level you are aiming for, you can make adjustments during the boil (see Tip 49). By adding sugar or sugar type, such as syrup or honey (see Tip 36), or by boiling the wort for a longer time, the sugar density will rise, which will result in a higher alcohol level. If the sugar density is too high, you can add water during the boil to decrease the sugar density.

ADDING SUGAR
Add the sugar or sugar type, if using, to the wort halfway through the boiling process. If added too early in the process, the sugar might caramelize.

49 BOIL THE WORT

When the correct volume of wort has been filtered into the boiling pot, it is time to start the boil. Bring the wort to a rolling boil, not a simmer, and maintain the rolling boil for 60–90 minutes, depending on the recipe. Don't forget to leave some headroom in the pot for the boiling water, as well as for adding the hops. If boiling particles, such as proteins, float to the surface during the boil, skim them off using a large spoon (see Tip 52).

HOT BREAK
The high temperature of the rolling boil creates a "hot break." This happens when proteins in the liquid are forced out of suspension, coagulate, then drop to the bottom of the boiling pot from where they can be easily removed.

50 BOILING FACTS

During the boiling process, the wort is sterilized, undesirable substances disappear, and proteins coagulate so that they can be easily removed. It is also during the boil that bitterness is added in the form of hops. When the water in the wort evaporates, the wort becomes concentrated, thereby increasing the sugar content and emphasizing the flavors. If boiled for a longer time, the wort caramelizes. This may be desirable for certain types of beer.

HOPS
Hops are added at various stages during the boil according to the recipe for that beer style. Depending on when they are added during the boil, they may impart bitterness, flavor, or aroma to the beer.

SUGAR
Sugar or sugar types are added halfway through the boil to adjust the alcohol level of the finished beer.

ADD THE HOPS

Use the tagged hop bags or bowls (see Tip 39) to add the hops according to the time specified in the recipe. Depending on the type of hop that is being added, and the time at which it is added, each hop addition has a different effect on the brew. If different hops are added at different stages of the boil, each of them lend their own flavor and aroma to the wort. If batches of the same hops are added at the beginning of the boil, they add bitterness, while later in the boil they add flavor and aroma.

FIRST-WORT HOPPING (FWH)

A traditional method is to add hops to the boiling pot and allow the runoff from the mash during sparging (see Tip 45) to gently pour over them. This allows the hops to steep and oxidize, allowing some of the aroma-giving beta acids to dissolve into the wort rather than being driven off due to boiling. Only aroma hops should be used in FWH, replacing some of those added at the end of the boil. This process increases the total bitterness of the beer slightly, without adding any harsh tones. However, it could make calculating the final bitterness level (IBU) of the beer more difficult.

HOPS FOR AROMA
Add any hops for aroma at the end of the boil.

Hops	Origin	Type	Flavor	Type of beer
Cascade	American	Aroma/Bitter	Citrus, grapefruit, spicy	Pale ale, IPA, Porter
East Kent Golding	British	Aroma	Flowery	British
Saaz	Czech	Aroma	Earthy, flowery, spicy	Belgian, Pilsner, Wheat
Centennial	American	Aroma/Bitter	Flowery, citrus	IPA, Ales
Fuggle	British	Aroma	Wood, fruity	British, Stout
Hallertauer	German	Aroma	Flowery, spicy	Pilsner, Bock, Lager
Amarillo	American	Bitter	Citrus	IPA, Ales

SKIM THE WORT

52 If you see any floating particles on the surface of the wort during the boil, skim them using a large spoon (see Tip 15). You can even use a sieve to do this. Skimming helps keep the wort as pure as possible, which helps later in the process. By removing the protein particles, the beer becomes clearer. However, be careful not to skim too deep or you may risk contaminating the wort.

WHAT IS SCUM MADE OF?

Most of the scum that floats to the surface of the wort is actually made up of compounds that come from the husks of malt added during mashing and from the hops.

SKIMMING EQUIPMENT

You can use a large spoon or a sieve to skim the scum from the surface of the wort.

Isinglass

CLEARING AFTER FERMENTATION

Clearing agents may also be added to the wort after fermentation (see Tip 62). This helps speed up the final stage of clearing and decrease the time taken for the beer to settle after transportation. Isinglass, produced from the swim bladder of fish, is a popular clearing agent used at that stage.

ADD THE CLEARING AGENT

53 Add the clearing agent when there are 15 minutes of boiling time left, according to the manufacturer's instructions. Most recipes will mention the amount of clearing agent to be added. Clearing agents cause the protein to flock (clump together), and slowly sink to the bottom, which prevents the particles from being carried over into the fermenter (see Tip 35).

COOL THE WORT

54 Let the wort boil the full time and then cool it down to 68–72°F (20–22°C) as quickly as possible. This is essential to avoid bacterial contamination and to prepare the wort for the next stage of fermentation (see Tip 62)—if the wort is too hot, the yeast cells will die when the yeast is added.

USING AN IMMERSION CHILLER
If using an immersion chiller, lower the chiller into the brew pot and pass cold water through it. Move the chiller around in the pot to maximize the cooling effect.

PREPARING AN ICE BATH
Take a tub or a bucket and fill one-third of it with water. Add ice cubes until the container is filled halfway. To cool the wort, place the boiling pot directly in the tub or bucket and leave until the wort cools down to 68°F (20°C).

COOLING METHODS

55 The three main methods to cool the wort are: using an ice bath, an immersion chiller, and a counterflow chiller, also known as a heat exchanger. An ice bath (see left) is both simple and cheap, but takes a long time to cool the wort. Because it is important to chill the wort as quickly as possible to reduce the risk of bacterial infection, an ice bath is not that effective. Using an immersion chiller (see Tips 27 and 54) can speed up the process significantly. Counterflow chillers, which work by using cold water to indirectly chill the wort, are even more effective than immersion chillers. There are two main types of counterflow chiller: the plate chiller, which has a number of stainless steel or copper plates that are brazed together, with cold water flowing through every alternate plate, and wort flowing through the rest; and the tube-inside-a-tube version where the inner tube is used for the wort and the outer for the water. The cold water in the plates or tubes helps cool the wort by flowing closely alongside it.

KEEP IT CLEAN

56 The boiling process has sterilized the wort. So, from this point onward, be extra careful with hygiene (see Tip 38) to avoid contaminating the wort.

SCRUB AWAY
Wash your hands with soap from time to time to make sure that any germs from your hands do not infect the wort.

FILTER THE WORT

57 After cooling, transfer the wort from the boiling pot to the fermenter. Remove the hop bags, if using, and use a large fine-mesh sieve (see Tip 17) to filter out particles from the wort as you pour it into the fermenter. Use the same sieve to filter a small amount of wort into a sterilized trial jar.

Glass fermenter

REMOVING HOP LEAVES
Using hop bags is the easiest way to remove the used hop leaves from the wort. However, even if you have not used hop bags, using a sieve can help filter out the hop leaves from the wort.

USING A FUNNEL
If you are using a glass fermenter with a small neck, use a funnel to avoid splashing the wort. Place the sieve on top of the funnel as you pour the wort into the fermenter.

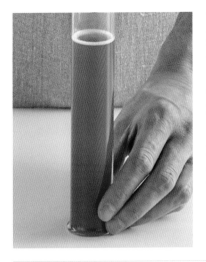

58 CONTROL WORT DENSITY AGAIN

Take a hydrometer and lower it into the trial jar filled with wort (see Tip 57). Take the reading in the same manner as before (see Tip 47). This reading is called OG, original gravity, and indicates the sugar level of the wort before fermentation. Take a note of the reading in order to calculate the alcohol content of the finished beer (see Tip 64).

SAMPLE VOLUME
Fill the trial jar to three-quarters of its total capacity. Any more and the jar may overflow when the hydrometer is placed into it.

59 AERATE THE WORT

Beat the wort vigorously with a large spoon or a balloon whisk to oxygenate it before the yeast is poured in. If using a glass carboy, cover its mouth with a loose-fitting cap, hold it tightly, and rock it back and forth to stir the wort. Yeast needs oxygen to multiply and do its job. However, this is the only time in the entire brewing process when the wort should be exposed to oxygen. If oxygen is in contact at any other time, the beer can spoil.

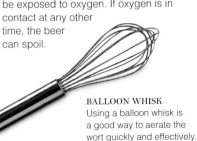

BALLOON WHISK
Using a balloon whisk is a good way to aerate the wort quickly and effectively.

FOAM LAYER
If using a plastic fermenter, whisk till you get at least 2–3in (5–8cm) of foam on top before you add the yeast.

41

ADD THE YEAST

60 Yeast comes in two forms: liquid and dried. Liquid yeast is poured into the wort; dried yeast is hydrated in a small quantity of boiled water cooled to 75°F (24°C) for 15 minutes prior to pitching. Adding the yeast to the wort, known as "pitching the yeast," is done when the yeast is at room temperature and the temperature of the wort is 68–72°F (20–22°C). After adding the yeast, stir gently with a sterilized spoon and put an airtight lid with an attached airlock (see Tip 61) on the fermenter.

USING LIQUID YEAST
If using liquid yeast, you may want to make a yeast starter before you add it to the fermenter (see Tip 83).

AIRLOCK

61 During the fermentation process, a large amount of carbon dioxide (CO_2) is created. An airlock, a one-way valve that is fitted to the top of the fermenter using a bung or rubber grommet, helps the carbon dioxide escape during the fermentation process, while not allowing air to enter, thus preventing oxidation.

Lid

Cup

Chamber

SIMPLE AIRLOCK
The simple airlock has a small plastic cup, which is filled with water or sanitizer, with a separate lid on top. The lid dislodges when pressure builds up inside the fermenter, allowing the carbon dioxide to escape. However, the cup stays on with the water inside, preventing the bacteria from entering and contaminating the wort.

BUBBLE AIRLOCK
A bubble airlock has a series of small chambers, which are filled with the mixed sterilizers (see Tip 12). The sterilizers prevent bacteria from the air from entering into the fermenter, while allowing the carbon dioxide to bubble out of it. The start of the bubbling is a hint that fermentation has begun.

FERMENTATION

62 At the fermentation stage, it is important to keep the wort at an even temperature—which is 64–75°F (18–24°C) for ales—so be aware of where you place the vessel. This does not mean that the temperature can vary between 64–75°F (18–24°C); instead, you should keep an even temperature as specified in the recipe. A lower temperature results in a cleaner-tasting beer while a higher temperature tends to add flavors to the beer, such as fruitiness, which may or may not be desired depending on your target beer type. Be careful to add the correct amount of yeast. It's always better to pitch too much yeast than too little since if you pitch too little, the fermenting process may remain incomplete.

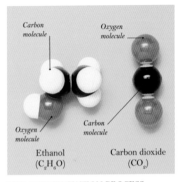

Ethanol (C_9H_6O)   Carbon dioxide (CO_2)

THE FERMENTATION PROCESS
During fermentation, the yeast cells multiply by feeding on the sugar. This process converts the sugar into alcohol (ethanol) and carbon dioxide.

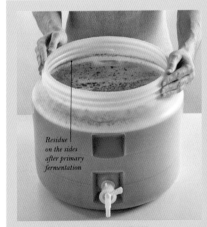

Residue on the sides after primary fermentation

ONE-VESSEL FERMENTATION
If only fermenting in one vessel, don't keep the beer for longer than three weeks, otherwise the dead yeast might develop off-flavors.

PRIMARY AND SECONDARY FERMENTATION
You should see activity, in the form of bubbles popping in the airlock and foam forming on the surface of the fermenter, within 8–24 hours after pitching the yeast. Leave the yeast to work from four to eight days, until you notice a decrease in activity in the airlock, for instance if the bubbles appear only once or twice per minute. This step is called primary fermentation. Now you can choose to either let the beer rest, mature, and clear for approximately another week and a half in the same vessel, or transfer the beer to a secondary airtight vessel for the remaining week and a half. Transferring the beer to a secondary fermenter can help remove any remaining grain particles, hop particles, or dead yeast cells that have accumulated at the bottom of the fermenter. If you choose to transfer the beer to a secondary vessel, be very careful not to splash the beer because you don't want it to be exposed to oxygen.

63 FERMENTATION TEMPERATURE

The main difference between lager and ale is the fermentation temperature and time. Lager uses a different kind of yeast, which ferments at a lower temperature (45–57°F/7–14°C), and therefore takes longer to ferment. Ale on the other hand ferments at a higher temperature, normally at 64–75°F (18–24°C), and takes a shorter time to ferment.

CHECK THE READING
To make sure the wort is at the correct temperature, use an external thermometer and attach it to the outside of the fermenter. This will help you take the temperature reading without disturbing the wort and introducing any risk of infection or oxidation.

64 MEASURE THE ALCOHOL CONTENT

ABV (alcohol by volume) is the measure used by most commercial brewers to measure the alcohol content of a brew. This figure tells you how much of the total volume of liquid is alcohol. Different beer types will have different ABVs, depending on what the original gravity (OG), and targeted final gravity (FG) of that beer type is.

CALCULATING ABV
To calculate the ABV (alcohol by volume) of your brew, take a hydrometer reading of the final wort after it has been fermented using the same procedure as before (see Tip 47). This third test gives the final gravity: FG. Subtract this from the second gravity measurement, OG (see Tip 58). Multiply the result by 131 to get the ABV of the beer. For example:

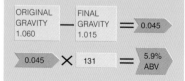

65 SAMPLE

Take a sample of the wort and taste it. This early sample will indicate what the finished beer will taste like, but it will still have traces of yeast and will most likely have rough edges to the flavor. These will all settle and the beer will mature and improve greatly with time through storage.

TASTING THE BEER
At this stage the wort is not carbonated, so be ready for a flat, somewhat warm beer.

66 TRANSFER THE WORT TO A CLEAN CONTAINER

After sampling the wort, transfer it to another vessel. Use a siphon, or, if the fermenter has a tap, use that to transfer the wort. Be careful not to splash or stir up the yeast and other sediments at the bottom of the fermenter. The wort should be exposed as little as possible to air, so don't stir the wort. The air will oxidize the wort and might give the beer a flat taste or even destroy the beer by enabling bacteria to spoil it.

Fermenter tap

USING A TAP
Fit a length of tubing to the tap (if your fermenter has one). Place the other end of the tubing into a sterilized container, and turn on the tap.

USING A SIPHON
Insert one end of a length of tubing into the top of the fermenter, and connect it to a siphon. Siphon the beer into a clean container, taking care not to disturb the yeast sediment at the bottom of the fermenter. Some siphons have a sediment trap that helps filter out the yeast debris (see Tip 25).

67 CARBONATE

Now it's time to prime the wort. Priming involves adding sugar to the wort to restart the fermentation in order to create carbon dioxide. You can use any type of sugar you want: corn sugar, cane sugar, or dried malt extract (DME). The amount of sugar required depends on the type of sugar being used, the size of the batch of beer, and the desired level of carbonation (see Tip 90). Instead of directly adding the sugar to the wort, it is best to make a priming solution by mixing the sugar with a little boiled water separately before adding it to the wort. Some home brewers add sugar directly to individual bottles after bottling, but this may introduce inconsistency in the level of carbonation among individual bottles as well as increase the risk of the bottle exploding if too much sugar has been added.

MAKING THE PRIMING SOLUTION

1 Measure 4–6½fl oz (100–200ml) water and pour it into a saucepan. Place the pan on the heat and bring it to a boil. Boil for 1–2 minutes to sterilize the water.

2 Measure the sugar (about ¼oz/5g sugar per quart of beer) and add it to the saucepan. Check the recipe for the exact amount of sugar you should add.

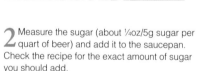

3 Using a spoon, stir the sugar mixture until the sugar dissolves in the water. Once it is ready, pour the mixture gently into the wort, stirring gently so the sugar is evenly distributed in the liquid. Make sure not to stir the wort too vigorously because no oxygen should be introduced into the beer at this stage.

68 BOTTLE THE WORT

Take the bottles you have cleaned and sterilized previously (see Tip 38) and fill them with the wort. You can use a siphon or a bottle-filling stick to bottle the wort or, if the vessel has a tap, you can fill up the bottles directly from the tap. Leave a headroom space of around ¾ in (2 cm) at the top of the bottles for carbonation.

USING A BOTTLE-FILLING STICK

A bottle-filling stick is a simple and convenient way to fill the beer bottles with the wort (see Tip 100). To fill the bottle, connect one end of a plastic tube to the vessel and one end to the bottle-filling stick. Insert the stick into the bottle, turn on the tap, and press down to release the valve. This starts the flow of beer into the bottle. The flow stops once you remove the stick from the bottle. Repeat for each bottle.

Valve

69 CAP THE BOTTLE

Once the bottle is filled, cap it immediately. Crown caps can be fixed using a manual bench crown capper or a twin lever capper (see Tip 28). Make sure all your caps have been sterilized before use.

USING A TWIN LEVER CAPPER

Slot a crown cap into the crown capper, then position the capper over the neck of the filled bottle. With equal pressure on both sides, push down both the levers firmly. Release the capper and check to make sure that the cap is secure.

70 STORE THE BEER BOTTLES

Store the bottles in a dark room at room temperature, at or above 62°F (17°C). Do not put them in the refrigerator immediately after bottling because the cold temperature will not allow the yeast to actively metabolize and create carbon dioxide, without which the beer will remain flat.

KEEP THEM UPRIGHT

Store the bottles upright to ensure that the yeast settles at the bottom of the beer bottle and, more importantly, it will also oxidize less, which means it will keep longer.

71 STORAGE TIME

Store the beers for a period of two to four weeks to allow carbon dioxide to form in the bottles. Then wait for another two to four weeks, depending on the beer style you are brewing, for the beer to mature and the foam to become heavier. Some home brewers put the beers in the refrigerator after the first two weeks. This may help the tannins, yeast, and protein to sediment faster, thus helping clear the beer more quickly. A well-brewed beer can last for more than a year if stored properly.

2 weeks

1 week

0 week

TIME IT

Allow at least 2 weeks primary storage to allow the beer to carbonate and develop a head and fizz.

ENJOY THE FINISHED RESULT

72

Now it is time to taste your first home-brewed beer and finally enjoy the fruits of your labor! There are two ways to pour your beer: with or without sediment. Most brewers prefer to pour it without the sediment (shown below). Once you have poured your beer, take a sip to see what it tastes like. Is it thick and creamy, or thin and light? Does it have the flavors you wished to incorporate into your brew? When analyzing the characteristics of the finished result, brewers tend to talk about mouthfeel and body of the beer. Mouthfeel involves three main attributes—carbonation, fullness, and afterfeel—and body generally refers to the thickness or weight of the beer. Try to understand the mouthfeel and body of your brew.

1 Tilt the glass slightly, at an angle of about 45°. Pour the beer in one smooth motion, filling two-thirds of the glass with the beer.

2 Straighten the glass and fill the final third without sediment to create a foam crown. The foam crown helps the beer's aroma come forth, and the color and texture also give additional clues about the beer's quality. Enjoy your drink!

RECIPES

73 CHOOSING BEER TYPE

If you are unsure of which type of beer to brew, there are a lot of websites on the Internet that can guide you. Style guides with suggested ingredients and relevant tips are also available if you want to create your own recipe. Once you choose the beer type, look for yeast and hop charts. These will provide information on what the finished beer will be like according to the yeast strain and hops you use. For example, using Wyeast Belgian ale with yeast number 1214 and two types of hops—Saaz hop (Czech) and Styrian Goldings—helps brew a fruity beer with no bitterness, such as the Belgian golden ale. Communities and forums on the Internet are also useful to get advice or troubleshoot once you start brewing.

COLOR CHART

The hue of the finished beer is measured using one of the three internationally recognized scales: European Brewing Convention (EBC), used for the recipes in this book, the Standard Reference Method (SRM), and Degrees Lovibond (°L). SRM is approximately equal to °L, EBC is equal to SRM multiplied by 1.97.

Recipes

75 PALE ALE
Style: American pale ale
• Type: All grain • Batch Size: 2½ gallons (10 liters) • Estimated Bottling Volume: 2½ gallons (9 liters) • Estimated Original Gravity: 1.050 SG • Estimated Final Gravity: 1.010 SG • Estimated Alcohol by Volume (ABV): 5.3% • Estimated Bitterness: 30 IBU • Estimated Color: 13 EBC

AMOUNT	INGREDIENT/TIMING	TYPE	%/IBU
2lb 15oz (1.3kg)	Pale ale malt (6 EBC)	Grain	54.2%
1lb 12oz (800g)	Pilsner malt (2 EBC)	Grain	33.3%
10½oz (300g)	Crystal malt (40 EBC)	Grain	12.5%
¾oz (10g)	Centennial [10% Alpha]—Boil 50 minutes	Hop	26 IBU
¼ tsp	Protafloc—Boil 15 minutes	Fining	
½oz (12g)	Cascade [5.5% Alpha]—Boil 15 minutes	Hop	9 IBU
¼oz (10g)	Cascade [5.5% Alpha]—Boil 5 minutes	Hop	3 IBU
1 packet	Dry yeast (Safale US-05)	Yeast	

MASH PROFILE		FERMENTATION
Method: Single infusion	Sparge: Fly sparge with 2½ gallons (9.1 liters) water at 168°F (75.5°C).	Primary fermentation: 66°F (19°C) for about 2 weeks.
Total water: 4 gallons/15.4 liters (mash in water 1½ gallons/6.3 liters, sparge water 2½ gallons/9.1 liters).		Alternative: 1 week primary fermentation and 2 weeks secondary fermentation.
	BOILING	
	Boil size: 3½ gallons (13 liters)	
MASH STEPS	End of boil volume: 2⅔ gallons (10.5 liters)	CARBONATION
Mash-in: Add 1¾ gallons (6.3 liters) water at 171°F (77°C), step temperature at 150°F (65.5°C) for 60 minutes.	Time: 60 minutes	Carbonation level: 2.3 volume of CO₂ = 2oz (48g) of table sugar for 2½ gallons (9 liters) of beer.
	Add hops and fining agent according to schedule.	

76 IPA
Style: India Pale Ale
• Type: All grain • Batch Size: 2⅝ gallons (10 liters) • Estimated Bottling Volume: 2⅝ gallons (9 liters) • Estimated Original Gravity: 1.061 SG • Estimated Final Gravity: 1.012 SG • Estimated Alcohol by Volume (ABV): 6.5% • Estimated Bitterness: 65.4 IBU • Estimated Color: 13.4 EBC

AMOUNT	INGREDIENT/TIMING	TYPE	%/IBU
3lb 3oz (1.6kg)	Pilsner malt (2 EBC)	Grain	55.2%
2lb 4oz (1 kg)	Pale ale malt (4 EBC)	Grain	34.5%
5½oz (150g)	Caraamber® (29 EBC)	Grain	5.2%
5½oz (150g)	Crystal malt (39.4 EBC)	Grain	5.2%
7g (¼oz)	Chinook [13% Alpha]—Boil 50 minutes	Hop	22.2 IBU
8g (¼oz)	Simcoe [13% Alpha]—Boil 30 minutes	Hop	20.5 IBU
¼ tsp	Protafloc—Boil 15 minutes	Fining	
¼oz (10g)	Citra [12% Alpha]—Boil 15 minutes	Hop	15.3 IBU
½oz (12g)	Citra [12% Alpha]—Boil 5 minutes	Hop	7.4 IBU
1 packet	Dry yeast (Safale US-05)	Yeast	

52

Ingredients/schedule
The quantity and type of ingredients required and the boiling schedule for the hops and fining agent. The %/IBU column specifies the percentage of a particular malt in the grain bill and the IBU rating of the hops used.

COLOR														
EBC	4	6	8	12	16	20	26	33	39	47	57	69	79	138
SRM/ LOVIBOND	2	3	4	6	8	10	13	17	20	24	29	35	40	70

74 HOW TO READ A RECIPE

All recipes in this book follow the common recipe format used by brewers. See below for an understanding of how to read a recipe.

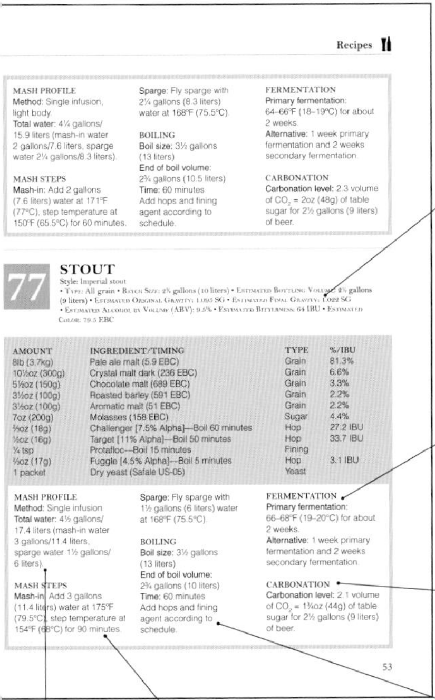

Recipes

MASH PROFILE
Method: Single infusion, light body.
Total water: 4¼ gallons/15.9 liters (mash-in water 2 gallons/7.6 liters, sparge water 2¼ gallons/8.3 liters).

MASH STEPS
Mash-in: Add 2 gallons (7.6 liters) water at 171°F (77°C), step temperature at 150°F (65.5°C) for 60 minutes.

Sparge: Fly sparge with 2¼ gallons (8.3 liters) water at 168°F (75.5°C).

BOILING
Boil size: 3½ gallons (13 liters)
End of boil volume: 2¾ gallons (10.5 liters)
Time: 60 minutes
Add hops and fining agent according to schedule.

FERMENTATION
Primary fermentation: 64–66°F (18–19°C) for about 2 weeks.
Alternative: 1 week primary fermentation and 2 weeks secondary fermentation.

CARBONATION
Carbonation level: 2.3 volume of CO_2 = 2oz (48g) of table sugar for 2½ gallons (9 liters) of beer.

77 STOUT

Style: Imperial stout
• Type: All grain • Batch Size: 2¾ gallons (10 liters) • Estimated Bottling Volume: 2½ gallons (9 liters) • Estimated Original Gravity: 1.095 SG • Estimated Final Gravity: 1.022 SG • Estimated Alcohol by Volume (ABV): 9.5% • Estimated Bitterness: 64 IBU • Estimated Color: 79.5 EBC

AMOUNT	INGREDIENT/TIMING	TYPE	%/IBU
8lb (3.7kg)	Pale ale malt (5.9 EBC)	Grain	81.3%
10½oz (300g)	Crystal malt dark (236 EBC)	Grain	6.6%
5½oz (150g)	Chocolate malt (689 EBC)	Grain	3.3%
3½oz (100g)	Roasted barley (591 EBC)	Grain	2.2%
3½oz (100g)	Aromatic malt (51 EBC)	Grain	2.2%
7oz (200g)	Molasses (158 EBC)	Sugar	4.4%
⅔oz (18g)	Challenger [7.5% Alpha]—Boil 60 minutes	Hop	27.2 IBU
½oz (16g)	Target [11% Alpha]—Boil 50 minutes	Hop	33.7 IBU
¼ tsp	Protafloc—Boil 15 minutes	Fining	
⅗oz (17g)	Fuggle [4.5% Alpha]—Boil 5 minutes	Hop	3.1 IBU
1 packet	Dry yeast (Safale US-05)	Yeast	

MASH PROFILE
Method: Single infusion
Total water: 4½ gallons/17.4 liters (mash-in water 3 gallons/11.4 liters, sparge water 1½ gallons/6 liters).

MASH STEPS
Mash-in: Add 3 gallons (11.4 liters) water at 175°F (79.5°C), step temperature at 154°F (68°C) for 90 minutes.

Sparge: Fly sparge with 1½ gallons (6 liters) water at 168°F (75.5°C).

BOILING
Boil size: 3½ gallons (13 liters)
End of boil volume: 2¾ gallons (10 liters)
Time: 60 minutes
Add hops and fining agent according to schedule.

FERMENTATION
Primary fermentation: 66–68°F (19–20°C) for about 2 weeks.
Alternative: 1 week primary fermentation and 2 weeks secondary fermentation.

CARBONATION
Carbonation level: 2.1 volume of CO_2 = 1¾oz (44g) of table sugar for 2½ gallons (9 liters) of beer.

53

Key information

Type: *The brewing method used (brewing kit, malt extract, or all grain, see Tip 10).*

Batch size: *The estimated volume of wort that reaches the fermenter after the wort has been boiled and chilled (the wort reduces by 4% when chilled and some is lost during the transfer to the fermenter, see Tips 54 and 57).*

Estimated bottling volume: *The estimated volume left to bottle after fermenting (the recipes in this book approximate a loss of 1¾ pints/1 liter in the yeast slurry and during bottling).*

Estimated original gravity (OG): *The estimated density of the wort after boiling (see Tip 58). SG is the specified gravity, which equals the density reading.*

Estimated final gravity (FG): *The estimated density of the wort after fermenting (see Tip 64).*

Estimated alcohol by volume (ABV): *The estimated alcohol content in the beer calculated from OG and FG (see Tip 64).*

Estimated bitterness: *The calculated bitterness of the beer (IBU=International Bittering Units).*

Estimated color: *The calculated color value of the beer (see Color chart, opposite).*

Fermentation

Primary fermentation: *The temperature at which the beer is fermented and the fermentation period (see Tip 62).*

Alternative: *If you go for secondary fermentation, this gives the time for which the beer should be kept for primary and secondary fermentation (see Tip 62).*

Carbonation

Carbonation level: *The level of carbon dioxide required in the beer (see Tip 90) and the amount of priming sugar required to create it (see Tip 67).*

Mash profile

Method: *The mashing process used (see Tip 81).*

Total water: *The total quantity of water required for mashing and sparging (see Tips 42 and 45).*

Mash steps

Mash-in: *The amount of water added to the mash tun, and the temperature it should be at (see Tip 41). Step temperature is the temperature of the water when malt is added to it (the temperature decreases).*

Sparge: *The amount of water added to sparge and the temperature it should be at when added to the mash tun (see Tip 45). Fly sparge is to sparge continuously.*

Boiling

Boil size: *The estimated volume of wort that should be transferred to the boiling pot (see Tip 49).*

End of boil volume: *The amount of wort that is left in the boiling pot after the boil.*

Time: *The total time period for which the wort is kept on a rolling boil. The hops and fining agent are added during this time (see Tips 51 and 53).*

PALE ALE

Style: American pale ale

• TYPE: All grain • BATCH SIZE: 2⅔ gallons (10 liters) • ESTIMATED BOTTLING VOLUME: 2½ gallons (9 liters) • ESTIMATED ORIGINAL GRAVITY: 1.050 SG • ESTIMATED FINAL GRAVITY: 1.010 SG • ESTIMATED ALCOHOL BY VOLUME (ABV): 5.3% • ESTIMATED BITTERNESS: 38 IBU • ESTIMATED COLOR: 13 EBC

AMOUNT	INGREDIENT/TIMING	TYPE	%/IBU
2lb 15oz (1.3kg)	Pale ale malt (6 EBC)	Grain	54.2%
1lb 12oz (800g)	Pilsner malt (2 EBC)	Grain	33.3%
10½oz (300g)	Crystal malt (40 EBC)	Grain	12.5%
¼oz (10g)	Centennial [10% Alpha]—Boil 50 minutes	Hop	26 IBU
¼ tsp	Protafloc—Boil 15 minutes	Fining	
½oz (12g)	Cascade [5.5% Alpha]—Boil 15 minutes	Hop	9 IBU
¼oz (10g)	Cascade [5.5% Alpha]—Boil 5 minutes	Hop	3 IBU
1 packet	Dry yeast (Safale US-05)	Yeast	

MASH PROFILE
Method: Single infusion
Total water: 4 gallons/
15.4 liters (mash-in water
1¾ gallons/6.3 liters, sparge
water 2½ gallons/9.1 liters).

MASH STEPS
Mash-in: Add 1¾ gallons
(6.3 liters) water at 171°F
(77°C), step temperature at
150°F (65.5°C) for 60 minutes.

Sparge: Fly sparge with
2½ gallons (9.1 liters)
water at 168°F (75.5°C).

BOILING
Boil size: 3½ gallons
(13 liters)
End of boil volume:
2¾ gallons (10.5 liters)
Time: 60 minutes
Add hops and fining agent
according to schedule.

FERMENTATION
Primary fermentation: 66°F
(19°C) for about 2 weeks.
Alternative: 1 week primary
fermentation and 2 weeks
secondary fermentation.

CARBONATION
Carbonation level: 2.3 volume
of CO_2 = 2oz (48g) of table
sugar for 2½ gallons (9 liters)
of beer.

IPA

Style: India Pale Ale

• TYPE: All grain • BATCH SIZE: 2⅔ gallons (10 liters) • ESTIMATED BOTTLING VOLUME: 2½ gallons (9 liters) • ESTIMATED ORIGINAL GRAVITY: 1.061 SG • ESTIMATED FINAL GRAVITY: 1.012 SG • ESTIMATED ALCOHOL BY VOLUME (ABV): 65% • ESTIMATED BITTERNESS: 65.4 IBU • ESTIMATED COLOR: 13.4 EBC

AMOUNT	INGREDIENT/TIMING	TYPE	%/IBU
3lb 3oz (1.6kg)	Pilsner malt (2 EBC)	Grain	55.2%
2lb 4oz (1 kg)	Pale ale malt (4 EBC)	Grain	34.5%
5½oz (150g)	Caraamber® (59 EBC)	Grain	5.2%
5½oz (150g)	Crystal malt (39.4 EBC)	Grain	5.2%
7g (¼oz)	Chinook [13% Alpha]—Boil 50 minutes	Hop	22.2 IBU
8g (¼oz)	Simcoe [13% Alpha]—Boil 30 minutes	Hop	20.5 IBU
¼ tsp	Protafloc—Boil 15 minutes	Fining	
¼oz (10g)	Citra [12% Alpha]—Boil 15 minutes	Hop	15.3 IBU
½oz (12g)	Citra [12% Alpha]—Boil 5 minutes	Hop	7.4 IBU
1 packet	Dry yeast (Safale US-05)	Yeast	

MASH PROFILE
Method: Single infusion,
light body.
Total water: 4¼ gallons/
15.9 liters (mash-in water
2 gallons/7.6 liters, sparge
water 2¼ gallons/8.3 liters).

MASH STEPS
Mash-in: Add 2 gallons
(7.6 liters) water at 171°F
(77°C), step temperature at
150°F (65.5°C) for 60 minutes.

Sparge: Fly sparge with
2¼ gallons (8.3 liters)
water at 168°F (75.5°C).

BOILING
Boil size: 3½ gallons
(13 liters)
End of boil volume:
2¾ gallons (10.5 liters)
Time: 60 minutes
Add hops and fining
agent according to
schedule.

FERMENTATION
Primary fermentation:
64–66°F (18–19°C) for about
2 weeks.
Alternative: 1 week primary
fermentation and 2 weeks
secondary fermentation.

CARBONATION
Carbonation level: 2.3 volume
of CO_2 = 2oz (48g) of table
sugar for 2½ gallons (9 liters)
of beer.

STOUT

Style: Imperial stout
• Type: All grain • Batch Size: 2¾ gallons (10 liters) • Estimated Bottling Volume: 2½ gallons
(9 liters) • Estimated Original Gravity: 1.095 SG • Estimated Final Gravity: 1.022 SG
• Estimated Alcohol by Volume (ABV): 9.5% • Estimated Bitterness: 64 IBU • Estimated
Color: 79.5 EBC

AMOUNT	INGREDIENT/TIMING	TYPE	%/IBU
8lb (3.7kg)	Pale ale malt (5.9 EBC)	Grain	81.3%
10½oz (300g)	Crystal malt dark (236 EBC)	Grain	6.6%
5½oz (150g)	Chocolate malt (689 EBC)	Grain	3.3%
3½oz (100g)	Roasted barley (591 EBC)	Grain	2.2%
3½oz (100g)	Aromatic malt (51 EBC)	Grain	2.2%
7oz (200g)	Molasses (158 EBC)	Sugar	4.4%
⅝oz (18g)	Challenger [7.5% Alpha]—Boil 60 minutes	Hop	27.2 IBU
½oz (16g)	Target [11% Alpha]—Boil 50 minutes	Hop	33.7 IBU
¼ tsp	Protafloc—Boil 15 minutes	Fining	
⅝oz (17g)	Fuggle [4.5% Alpha]—Boil 5 minutes	Hop	3.1 IBU
1 packet	Dry yeast (Safale US-05)	Yeast	

MASH PROFILE
Method: Single infusion
Total water: 4½ gallons/
17.4 liters (mash-in water
3 gallons/11.4 liters,
sparge water 1½ gallons/
6 liters).

MASH STEPS
Mash-in: Add 3 gallons
(11.4 liters) water at 175°F
(79.5°C), step temperature at
154°F (68°C) for 90 minutes.

Sparge: Fly sparge with
1½ gallons (6 liters) water
at 168°F (75.5°C).

BOILING
Boil size: 3½ gallons
(13 liters)
End of boil volume:
2¾ gallons (10 liters)
Time: 60 minutes
Add hops and fining
agent according to
schedule.

FERMENTATION
Primary fermentation:
66–68°F (19–20°C) for about
2 weeks.
Alternative: 1 week primary
fermentation and 2 weeks
secondary fermentation.

CARBONATION
Carbonation level: 2.1 volume
of CO_2 = 1¾oz (44g) of table
sugar for 2½ gallons (9 liters)
of beer.

78 STRONG ALE

Style: Strong Scottish ale

• Type: All grain • Batch Size: 2¾ gallons (10 liters) • Estimated Bottling Volume: 2½ gallons (9 liters) • Estimated Original Gravity: 1.099 SG • Estimated Final Gravity: 1.026 SG • Estimated Alcohol by Volume (ABV): 9.6% • Estimated Bitterness: 26 IBU • Estimated Color: 40.4 EBC

AMOUNT	INGREDIENT/TIMING	TYPE	%/IBU
8lb (3.6kg)	Pale ale malt (6 EBC)	Grain	7.8%
2lb 1oz (600g)	Crystal malt (40 EBC)	Grain	12.6%
1lb (500g)	Melanoiden malt (40 EBC)	Grain	10.5%
1lb (500g)	Chocolate malt (885 EBC)	Grain	1.1%
¼oz (8g)	Challenger [7.5% Alpha]—Boil 60 minutes	Hop	11.8 IBU
¼oz (10g)	E.K. Goldings [5% Alpha]—Boil 30 minutes	Hop	7.5 IBU
⅓oz (11g)	Fuggle [4.5% Alpha]—Boil 20 minutes	Hop	5.9 IBU
¼ tsp	Protafloc—Boil 15 minutes	Fining	
¼oz (5g)	E. K. Goldings [5% Alpha]—Boil 5 minutes	Hop	1 IBU
1 packet	Scottish ale (Wyeast #1728)	Yeast	

MASH PROFILE

Method: Single infusion
Total water: 4¾ gallons/17.8 liters (mash-in water 3¼ gallons/12.4 liters, sparge water 1½ gallons/5.4 liters).

MASH STEPS

Mash-in: Add 3¼ gallons (12.4 liters) water at 171°F (77°C), step temperature at 152.5°F (67°C) for 60 minutes.
Sparge: Fly sparge with 1½ gallons (5.4 liters) water at 168°F (75.5°C).

BOILING

Boil size: 3½ gallons (13 liters)
End of boil volume: 2¾ gallons (10.5 liters)
Time: 60 minutes
Add hops and fining agent according to schedule.

FERMENTATION

Primary fermentation: 66°F (19°C) for about 2 weeks.
Alternative: 1 week primary fermentation and 2 weeks secondary fermentation.

CARBONATION

Carbonation level: 2.1 volume of CO_2 = 1³⁄₄oz (44g) of table sugar for 2½ gallons (9 liters) of beer.

LAGER

Style: Modern lager
• Type: All grain • Batch Size: 2¾ gallons (10 liters) • Estimated Bottling Volume: 2½ gallons (9 liters) • Estimated Original Gravity: 1.054 SG • Estimated Final Gravity: 1.013 SG • Estimated Alcohol by Volume (ABV): 5.4% • Estimated Bitterness: 30.4 IBU • Estimated Color: 10 EBC

AMOUNT	INGREDIENT/TIMING	TYPE	%/IBU
4¾ lb (2.2kg)	Pilsner malt (3.9 EBC)	Grain	88%
10½oz (300g)	Munich malt (19.7 EBC)	Grain	12%
¼oz (6g)	Amarillo [9.2% Alpha]—Boil 60 minutes	Hop	14.8 IBU
¼oz (5g)	Amarillo [9.2% Alpha]—Boil 20 minutes	Hop	7.5 IBU
¼oz (5g)	Cascade [5.5% Alpha]—Boil 20 minutes	Hop	4.5 IBU
¼ tsp	Protafloc—Boil 15 minutes	Fining	
¼oz (5g)	Amarillo [9.2% Alpha]—Boil 5 minutes	Hop	2.5 IBU
¼oz (6g)	Cascade [5.5% Alpha]—Boil 3 minutes	Hop	1.1 IBU
1 packet	Dry Yeast (Safale lager)	Yeast	

MASH PROFILE
Method: Single infusion
Total water: 4 gallons/15.5 liters (mash-in water 1¾ gallons/6.5 liters, sparge water 2½ gallons/9 liters).

MASH STEPS
Mash-in: Add 1¾ gallons (6.5 liters) water at 173°F (78.5°C), step temperature at 152.5°F (67°C) for 60 minutes.
Sparge: Fly sparge with 2½ gallons (9 liters) water at 168°F (75.5°C).

BOILING
Boil size: 3½ gallons (13 liters)
End of boil volume: 2¾ gallons (10.5 liters)
Time: 60 minutes
Add hops and fining agent according to schedule.

FERMENTATION
Fermentation: 50°F (10°C) for about 3 weeks.

CARBONATION
Carbonation level: 2.3 volume of CO_2 = 2oz (48g) of table sugar for 2½ gallons (9 liters) of beer.

THE NEXT LEVEL

80 WATER TREATMENT AND QUALITY

The chemical makeup of the water you use is crucial for the type of beer you want to brew. For instance, soft water is better suited for lager while hard water is better for stout. If you want to brew a higher quality beer, you can ask your local water authority to provide you with a water quality report and, based on the report, you can treat the water to adjust for any deficiencies. For example, the water can be treated with salts and other chemicals to make it suitable for the desired beer type. If the water is of very poor quality, you can even buy distilled water, which is neutral, and mix it with a proportion of your local tap water, to use it for brewing.

THE PERFECT STOUT
Stouts are best brewed using hard alkaline water, which is high in minerals.

TREATING WATER

A few of the substances commonly used to treat water include calcium sulfate, calcium chloride, magnesium sulfate, calcium carbonate, and lactic acid. These are used to regulate the mineral content, pH level, and softness or hardness of the water.

Calcium chloride
(in powdered form)

Magnesium sulfate

Calcium carbonate

MASHING METHODS

81 There are three main mashing methods: decoction mashing, temperature mashing, and infusion mashing. In decoction mashing, the wort is heated in installments. To do this, heat up a portion of the mash at a time and pour it back into the remaining wort to quickly heat up the total amount of wort. In temperature mashing, the mash tun is heated up using an electric element, or on a stove, to raise or maintain the mash temperature. In infusion mashing, the temperature is maintained by adding additional hot water. All three methods can be used for single mashing, where a specific temperature is maintained throughout the mashing process, or for multi-rest mashing, where temperature stops, called "rests," are made at certain intervals during the mashing process, for a certain period of time, such as the saccharification rest, acid rest, and protein rest. The saccharification rest is necessary because in this rest, starch is converted into fermentable and unfermentable sugars; without it there is no beer.

INSULATED MASHING VESSEL
Use an insulated mashing vessel such as this to help maintain the specified mashing temperature. If you are using any other vessel, wrap a foam mat around it to insulate it.

DIFFERENT YEAST STRAINS AND THEIR CHARACTERISTICS

82 Several yeast strains are available on the market, each with different flavor characteristics, mouthfeel, and body, as well as different optimal fermentation temperature and alcohol tolerances. Select a yeast strain that is suited to the beer style you are aiming to brew. For instance, if you wish to brew a beer with a high alcohol content, use a yeast strain that can handle the targeted alcohol

level. Also consider attenuation and flocculation. Attenuation is how much sugar the yeast is able to consume. Low attenuation yeasts create maltier beers, while high attenuation yeasts create drier, less sweet beers. Flocculation is the ability of the yeast to clump together. Higher flocculation yeast fall quickly to the bottom of the fermenter, helping to clear the beer faster.

FERMENTING TEMPERATURE
While fermenting, make sure you maintain the correct temperature for your chosen yeast strain as specified by the manufacturer.

83 YEAST CULTURING

Some home brewers propagate their own yeast. This helps keep costs down and ensures that you have the most viable yeast available. The disadvantages with culturing your own yeast is the time it takes for developing the yeast as well as the extra equipment required. If you are culturing your own yeast, be careful to maintain the temperature at around 68°F (20°C) during the cultivation. If the temperature is lower the yeast will be ineffective, while a higher temperature might stress the yeast and produce unwanted esters.

1 Boil about ½ pint (500ml) water, depending on the amount of yeast you require, in an Erlenmeyer flask (see Tip 97). Pour the malt extract into the boiling water, and boil for another 10 minutes until it blends into the water.

2 Let the mixture cool down to about 68°F (20°C) rapidly in ice water. Add the yeast, then give the flask a good shake for 1 minute.

3 Seal the flask using a sterilized rubber stopper with an airlock, or aluminum foil, to avoid contamination. After 1–2 days, foam will cover the surface of the yeast, indicating that it has started multiplying. Maintain the temperature at around 68°F (20°C) during this process.

4 Leave the yeast culture for another day at most, until the foam has settled, then add the yeast culture to the fermenter.

USING A BELT HEATER

Wrap the belt around the fermentation vessel to raise the temperature. Slide it up or down the vessel to alter the temperature as required.

USING A HEAT PAD

Place the heat pad on the floor and then position the fermenter on top of it. The heat pad heats up to a set temperature above the ambient temperature.

84 FERMENTATION HEATING METHODS

Each yeast strain has its own optimal fermentation temperature—make sure you maintain the temperature in your fermenting bin at that level. If the fermentation temperature goes above the optimal, it may introduce off-flavors; if it goes below the optimal, it may stall the fermentation process. To increase the fermentation temperature, use a heat pad or a belt heater. An immersion heater, which is submerged inside the wort is also an effective way to heat up the wort. Preferably, use these in conjunction with a universal thermostat (see Tip 86).

85 FERMENTATION COOLING METHODS

Some beer types, such as lagers, require a lower temperature of around 45–67°F (7–14°C) to ferment (see Tip 63). If the temperature goes above this range, it can introduce off-flavors in the beer. A refrigerator is very useful for controlling the temperature if it goes above the acceptable range. A refrigerator can also be useful in cold crashing the beer at the end of fermentation (see Tip 87). It helps to quickly cool down the wort to a low temperature to help clarify the beer.

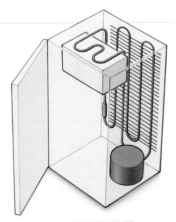

MAKING SPACE

Remove the refrigerator shelves to make room for your fermenter or carboy.

86 FERMENTATION TEMPERATURE CONTROL

The fermentation temperature of various devices can be controlled using a universal thermostat—an electric device with a temperature-controlled relay to switch the temperature on and off. If using a hot plate for mashing, the power can be turned on and off at a specific temperature controlled by a universal thermostat. Likewise the thermostat can be used to control the temperature of a refrigerator during fermentation (see Tip 85) or during cold crashing (see Tip 87), or for controlling a heat pad during fermentation (see Tip 84).

Refrigerator

87 FERMENTATION TIPS

Apart from a particular style and flavor, all home brewers aim to create a clean-tasting and clean-looking beer. A few additional procedures, such as cold crashing and diacetyl rest (see below), can be used during fermentation to refine the fermentation and conditioning process, and produce a more perfect end result.

Beer after primary fermentation

COLD CRASHING

It is advisable to cold crash the beer after the secondary fermentation (see Tip 62). Place the beer in a refrigerator at a temperature of 32–41°F (0–5°C) for 1–3 days. The yeast and protein particles will clot together and fall to the bottom of the fermenter. Then transfer the clean beer to another container, leaving the sediments behind (see Tip 66).

DIACETYL REST

At the end of the primary fermentation process (see Tip 62), increase the temperature by 34–36°F (1–2°C) and leave the beer for 1–2 days to allow the yeast to remove diacetyl, characterized by a butterscotch aroma and flavor, and create a cleaner-tasting beer.

88 ADDITIONAL FLAVORS AND SPICES

You can add additional ingredients to your beer to enhance or change its taste, including chocolate, coffee, whiskey, herbs, flowers, spices, berries, and fruits. To give your beer an oak character, use oak cubes and add them after fermentation. You can also use oak barrels during fermentation to add the oak flavor, but they pose a greater risk of infecting the beer because they are difficult to clean.

COCOA

Cocoa works well with brown ales, porters, and stouts. It has a bittersweet chocolate flavor. Use chocolate syrup, cocoa powder, cocoa nibs, or cocoa beans.

CHERRIES

For a cherry flavor, add fresh cherries, cherry juice, or juice concentrate to the beer. Cherries work well with Belgian, wheat, and sour beers.

LEMON

Lemon lends a citrus note to wheat beers, pale American lagers, pilsners, IPAs, and stouts. Use the juice of the lemon, or use lemon jam, lemon peel or zest, or its oil.

ELDERFLOWERS

These work well with IPAs, Belgian beers, wheat beers, sour beers, and pilsners. They lend a tart fruit note to the beer. Use fresh or dried.

COFFEE

Coffee gives a bitter, roast note, and a coffee flavor to pale ales, stouts, porters, and lagers. Add whole beans, or use ground or brewed coffee.

CHILI PEPPERS

Chili peppers work well with ales, stouts, and pilsners, lending a subtle spicy flavor. Use them fresh, dried, or as a juice or oil.

89 DRY HOPPING

Dry hopping is the process of adding hops to the beer after fermentation is complete. These hops are additional to the ones already added during the brewing process (see Tip 51). Dry hopping is a common technique and is used to enhance the hoppy aroma of the beer to create citrus, floral, or other tones. There are several different methods for dry hopping but the easiest, cheapest, and most common method is to add hop cobs to the beer once primary fermentation is complete (see Tip 62). The hops should ideally stay in the beer for a couple of days but it depends on the recipe. The amount of hops you add to the beer will also depend on the recipe you are following.

DRY HOPPING USING A HOPBACK

You can also dry hop using a hopback—a small, insulated vessel filled with whole leaf hops. After the boil and before you cool the wort (see Tip 54), connect one vent of the hopback to the boiling pot and the other to the wort chiller. Then pump warm wort through the hop-filled container and into the wort chiller. This adds aroma and flavor from the hops into the wort.

NO BITTERNESS

Because the hops are not boiled during dry hopping, they only add flavor and aroma to the beer, not bitterness.

DRY HOPPING ESSENTIALS

• Make sure that the container to which you are adding the hops has sufficient space at the top, because the hops tend to expand once added to the beer.

• Keep the hops in a muslin or nylon hop bag when dry hopping in order to make them easier to remove afterward.

• Avoid using hop pellets for dry hopping because they are difficult to retrieve.

CARBONATION METHODS

90

There are three methods of carbonating beer: priming, carbonating with gas, and carbonating naturally. Priming is adding sugar to the beer after fermentation. This makes the yeast referment and create carbon dioxide (see Tip 67). Carbonating with gas is when you attach a gas cylinder to a beer keg and force-carbonate it (see Tip 91). Make sure you check the required gas pressure, which will vary according to the temperature of the beer and the volume of carbon dioxide desired. For carbonating naturally, a pressure tank, also called a "combo tank" (a combined fermentation and pressure tank) is used during fermentation. When carbon dioxide builds up inside the tank, the pressure is adjusted through the pressure vent so that the carbon dioxide goes back into the wort, thereby carbonating it naturally.

CARBONATION LEVEL
Every beer must have the right level of carbonation when served. This gives it the tingle and effervescence associated with beer.

CARBONATION LEVEL
The carbonation level of a beer is measured as volume of carbon dioxide (CO_2). This measurement is a relative description of how much gas is dissolved in the beer. Carbonation levels differ between various beer types. Belgian beers, for example, are highly carbonated, while draft beers usually have low carbonation levels. See below for the recommended CO_2 volume for some beer types:

British ales:	Lagers:	American ales:	Wheat beers:
1.3–2.3 volume of CO_2	2.3–2.7 volume of CO_2	2.0–2.8 volume of CO_2	3.0–4.2 volume of CO_2

91
CARBONATION EQUIPMENT

The equipment recommended when force-carbonating (see Tip 90) is a cylinder of carbon dioxide fitted with a gas regulator, or a counter pressure bottle filler or beer gun. The gas cylinder is connected to the beer keg with a hose through which gas is passed into the keg. The gas regulator usually has two gauges: one shows the pressure of gas in the cylinder and the other displays the pressure of gas in the beer keg. If carbonating a bottle, a counter pressure bottle filler makes the process quicker, cleaner, and avoids exposing the beer to excessive oxygen. A nozzle attached to a gas cylinder at one end and to a beer barrel at the other end transfers beer under pressure to the bottle through two separate hoses. A beer gun (see Tip 100) works in a similar manner. Gas cylinders come in different sizes and can be changed or refilled at a regular store or gas station.

92
KEGS AND CASKS

Aside from bottles, beer can also be stored in kegs and casks. A keg is a big container used to store and serve beer under pressure. Kegs and casks can be made of either plastic or metal. They are more expensive to purchase than bottles and you will also require a canister of carbon dioxide with a fitted regulator to carbonate the brew. Compared to kegs and casks, bottles are easy to store and the beer lasts for several months in them. Bottles also retain carbonation well, although it takes a long time to clean and sterilize them, and to fill them with the beer. Kegs and casks, on the contrary, are easier to clean and less quantity of beer is wasted when transferring beer to a keg or cask.

CORNELIUS KEG
This popular keg is ideal for serving highly carbonated beer.

PRESSURE BARRELS
Pressure barrels are large plastic containers that can hold up to 6½ gallons (25 liters) of beer. They are inexpensive, easy to clean, and the beer will usually keep for weeks in them. They are fitted with a tap, so no additional equipment is required for serving. A vent at the top allows the brew to vent if the pressure goes above its capacity. Priming sugar (see Tip 67) is added to the beer prior to barreling. As the beer is drunk and pressure decreases, additional carbon dioxide can be added via a valve. However, pressure barrels need to be stored in a cool place or refrigerator to serve beer at the right temperature, and it can become difficult to control the level of carbonation.

93 BREWING SOFTWARE

Brewing software is invaluable when you want to create your own recipes or keep track of your progress. A number of computer software programs and applications are now available that provide data on water treatment, precultivation, carbonation, and other brewing processes, and help you record your costs, calculate recipes, and so on. Many applications also create worksheets that can help you plan your brewing day. Some even help you calculate brewhouse efficiency, to determine how efficient your equipment is.

MOBILE APPLICATIONS
A number of brewing applications that can be run on mobile phones are also available, giving mobility and flexibility to the home brewer.

94 MALT MILLS

A malt mill is essential equipment if you want a wider range of malt. It also allows you to decide for yourself how the grain will be crushed by setting the roller distance. Having a malt mill ensures that you always have freshly milled grain whenever you start brewing. There are two main types of malt mills. The first is based on a corn mill known as a "Corona," and although it is the least expensive, it is slow to use and produces poor results. Specifically, the malt is often ground rather than milled, which causes problems during mashing (see Tip 40). The second variant is a two- or three-roller mill, which provides greater precision. It also allows you to set the distance between the rollers so that the grains are crushed according to your preference. This is more costly, but also more efficient.

ROLL OVER THE GRAIN
If brewing a small batch of beer using dried or liquid malt extract, a rolling pin is a cheap and effective option to crush the small amount of grains required. Simply place the grains in a plastic bag and seal it, then roll the rolling pin over the bag till the grain is milled.

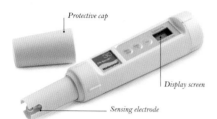

Protective cap

Display screen

Sensing electrode

DIGITAL pH TESTER
A digital pH tester is simple to use and easy to calibrate. It is also easier to read and more accurate, particularly if it measures up to +/- 0.01 pH.

95 pH METER

A pH meter is an instrument used to measure acidity and basicity during mashing. The reason why it's important to measure the pH when brewing is because yeast thrives in a pH range of 5.1–5.4. The closer the pH is to this range, the more complete the fermentation will be. If you don't have a pH meter, you can use litmus paper strips for this test.

pH TESTER STRIPS
pH tester strips are commonly available and are inexpensive—just dip them in the liquid you want to test. However, pH strips are difficult to read because the color needs to be matched to a color chart and sometimes the difference between two readings is so insignificant, it is difficult to tell them apart.

96 MAGNETIC STIRRER

A magnetic stirrer is a laboratory device used to propagate the yeast before adding it to the wort (see Tip 83). The flask with the yeast slurry is placed on top of the magnetic stir plate and a stir bar is placed inside the flask, in the yeast slurry. When switched on, a magnetic field makes the stir bar inside the flask rotate rapidly, creating a vortex that introduces air into the yeast slurry. This helps the yeast multiply more rapidly.

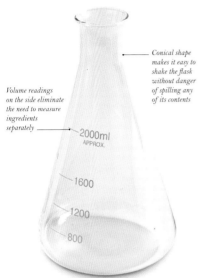

Conical shape makes it easy to shake the flask without danger of spilling any of its contents

Volume readings on the side eliminate the need to measure ingredients separately

2000ml
APPROX.

1600

1200

800

97 ERLENMEYER FLASK

An Erlenmeyer flask is a conical vessel made of heat-resistant glass. It is used to propagate yeast (see Tip 83). The advantage is that you can use it to combine ingredients, heat up its contents, and ferment the yeast, so you don't need separate vessels for different processes. Be sure to use a flask large enough for the amount you are brewing. When using it to ferment the yeast, seal its mouth with a rubber stopper provided with an airlock to prevent the yeast from getting infected.

98 FERMENTERS

Use a plastic or stainless steel fermenter during fermentation (see Tip 62). Stainless steel fermenters are more expensive than the plastic ones, though both work equally well. Conical fermenters that have an extended cone at the bottom are also available. These are especially useful, because the yeast collects at the bottom of the cone and can be easily disposed off, or reused for pitching into a new batch.

CHOOSING A FERMENTER
If buying a plastic fermenter, choose a model that can withstand scratches to avoid bacterial growth.

99 REFRACTOMETER

A refractometer is an optical instrument that measures the density of a liquid, just as a hydrometer does (see Tip 20). The difference between the two is that a refractometer cannot measure the density of the beer, only the wort, while a hydrometer can do both. However, it is considerably faster to take a reading on a refractometer than on a hydrometer.

Optical prism

USING A REFRACTOMETER
Add a few drops of the liquid to the refractometer's optical prism, and allow them to cool to room temperature. The device will display the density reading.

100 BOTTLE-FILLING METHODS

A number of options are available for filling up bottles with your home-brewed beer, such as using a bottle-filling stick or a beer gun. A bottle-filling stick is a hollow plastic stick with a valve at its tip. It releases beer on demand (see Tip 68). A beer gun, as its name indicates, is a kind of gun that has a trigger to regulate the flow of beer and is fitted with a valve at the bottom of the filler to avoid foaming. Beer guns also serve a second purpose, that of replacing the air in the bottle with carbon dioxide, which helps avoid oxidation. Exposing the beer to oxygen will develop off-flavors, as well as shorten its lifetime. You can also siphon the beer into a new container fitted with a tap, and fill up the bottles directly from the tap. Be careful to avoid moving the wort too much to avoid oxidation. Leave the yeast and other sediments behind when siphoning.

BOTTLE-FILLING STICK
The bottle-filling stick allows you to stop the flow of beer and restart it at will. This helps avoid overfilling the bottle and allows you to move from one bottle to the next without spilling.

101 LABELING

It is fun to create your own bottle labels, and personalized beer bottles can be a popular house present or gift, or if you want to make a little extra effort for a special event. It can also be valuable for future brewing to include dates when the beer was produced, the beer type, volume, ingredients, hop variety, how it was stored, OG (original gravity of the beer, see Tip 58), ABV percentage (see Tip 64), and IBU rating (IBU = International Bitterness Unit, a measure of the bitterness of a beer). This way you can differentiate your beer bottles from different batches, and it will be easier to re-create the same result in the future. If you don't have the imagination to design your own label, a number of label templates are available on the Internet that can be used. The easiest way to print the labels is to buy adhesive labels, and use a laser printer to print them out (labels printed on inkjet printers are not colorfast).

1 Create a design. You can use your own imagination, or select a label template from the Internet. Include any additional information you want on the label. It may also be interesting to give a name to your brew.

2 Print the labels out on adhesive label sheets. Hold the bottle in one hand and use the other hand to position the label over the bottle. Press the label down gently, smoothing it over the bottle.

OTHER LABEL IDEAS
You can also look at some of these labels for inspiration, and add any additional information about the beer on them as suggested above.

INDEX

ACKNOWLEDGMENTS

Dorling Kindersley would like to thank the following for their kind
permission to reproduce their photographs:
(Key: a-above; b-below/bottom; c-center; f-far; l-left; r-right; t-top)

12 Dorling Kindersley: Michael Jackson (bc). 49 Dorling Kindersley:
Michael Jackson (cl, br). 56 Dorling Kindersley: The Science Museum,
London (br)

All other images © Dorling Kindersley
For further information see: www.dkimages.com

Additional credits
Dorling Kindersley would like to thank Hilary Bird for creating the index for
this book.